COMMUNITY HELPERS

FIREFIGHTERS

Written by
Eliza Nodes

Genius Kid

sales@northstareditions.com | 888-417-0195

Library of Congress Control Number:
2025943068

ISBN
979-8-89471-051-8 (library bound)
979-8-89471-071-6 (paperback)
979-8-89471-110-2 (epub)
979-8-89471-091-4 (hosted ebook)

Printed in the United States of America
Mankato, MN
012026

Written by:
Eliza Nodes

Edited by:
Rebecca Phillips-Bartlett

Designed by:
Ker Ker Lee

All facts, statistics, web addresses, and URLs in this book were verified as valid and accurate at time of writing. No responsibility for any changes to external websites or references can be accepted by either the author or publisher.

Photo Credits – Images courtesy of Shutterstock.com, unless otherwise stated.

Cover – Egor Tetiushev, Pixel-Shot, Phaphthay, JANNTA, Nikolai Tsvetkov, My name is boy, CHARTGRAPHIC, PrasongTakham, GSPstock, GSPstock, Teerapong mahawan. 2–3 – kckate16, serhii.suravikin, KUSHEI. 4–5 – serhii.suravikin, Shakirov Albert. 6–7 – MyCreationWorld, ChiccoDodiFC, VAKS-Stock Agency. 8–9 – Flashon Studio, VAKS-Stock Agency, Ljupco Smokovski, Tyler Olson. 10–11 – creativesunday, serhii. suravikin Dusan Petkovic, Rob Wilson. 12–13 – Michael Derrer Fuchs, symbiot, BigTunaOnline. 14–15 – AdriaVidal, K-FK, bundit jonwises. 16–17 – Morphart Creation, Gold Picture, Everett Collection. 18–19 – Levent Konuk, Ritu Manoj Jethani, ChiccoDodiFC. 20–21 – Everett Collection, Flashon Studio, Eric Isselee, Bere Regis, fire hooks, taken Thursday, 23 April, 2009 cc-by-sa/2.0 - © Mike Faherty. 22–23 – Roman Samborskyi, Vanessa van Rensburg, serhii.suravikin, SanchaiRat, studioloco, Sichon.

CONTENTS

Words that look like this can be found in the glossary on page 24.

FIREFIGHTERS

When you hear the word *firefighter*, what do you imagine?

Do you picture a bright red truck? Or maybe you see a person wearing a helmet and carrying a hose?

Firefighters are important members of the community. They help keep people and animals safe.

Many people think that a firefighter's only job is to put out fires. However, firefighters also help those who are injured or in danger for many other reasons.

MANY JOBS IN ONE

Firefighters do many different jobs.

FIGHTING FIRES

Firefighters are called when there's a fire. Fires need oxygen, fuel, and heat to start. Firefighters stop fires by getting rid of one of these elements.

DID YOU KNOW?

Fuel is anything that can be burned as a source of energy.

RESCUING OTHERS

Firefighters rescue people and animals who are stuck. Rescues may take place in water or high places. Firefighters also help during car crashes and natural disasters.

PROVIDING CARE

Firefighters are trained in first aid. They also need to be kind and comforting to people who are hurt or scared.

WRITING REPORTS

It's a firefighter's job to figure out what caused each fire. They write what they have found in a report for the police.

TEACHING THE COMMUNITY

Many firefighters go to schools and workplaces to teach fire safety. This includes teaching others about fire alarms and fire extinguishers.

STAYING IN SHAPE

Firefighters must be fit and strong. They use exercise equipment to stay in shape.

CHECKING EQUIPMENT

Every day, firefighters check to make sure their gear is working properly. They also check each piece of equipment on the fire engines.

AT THE FIRE STATION

Firefighters work at fire stations.

DORMS

Many firefighters work for 24 hours straight. They sleep in large bedrooms called dorms in between emergencies.

DID YOU KNOW?

Older fire stations have poles for firefighters to slide down. However, some modern fire stations don't have poles.

ALARMS

A dispatcher alerts firefighters by sounding an alarm. The dispatcher tells the firefighters what and where the emergency is.

FIRE ENGINES

Fire engines are stored at the fire station. They have lights and sirens so people can see and hear them coming.

EQUIPMENT

Firefighters use many kinds of equipment to put out fires.

Firefighters use hoses to spray water on fires. Hoses come in different sizes. Some hoses are so big that they need two firefighters to control them.

DID YOU KNOW?
Fire hoses were invented around 1673.

Ladders are stored on top of the fire engines. They help firefighters reach places up high. Some ladders are more than 43 feet (13 m) long.

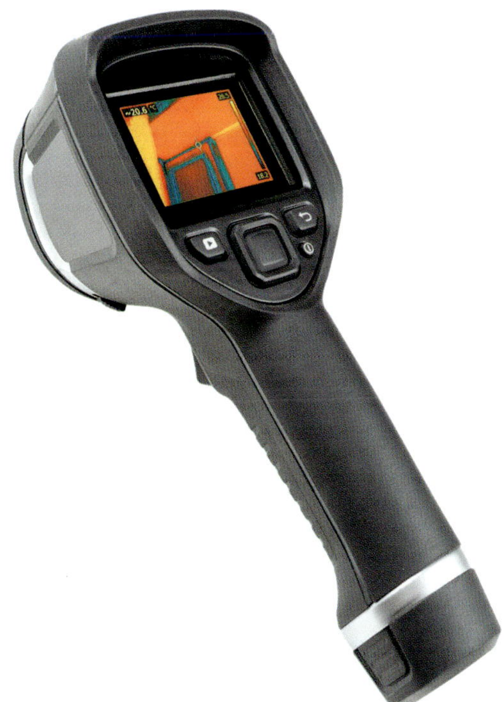

Thermal imaging cameras pick up heat. Firefighters use them to track fires and find people inside buildings.

Fireproof jackets and pants protect firefighters from the heat of a fire. They also protect firefighters' skin from harmful chemicals that may be in the air during a fire.

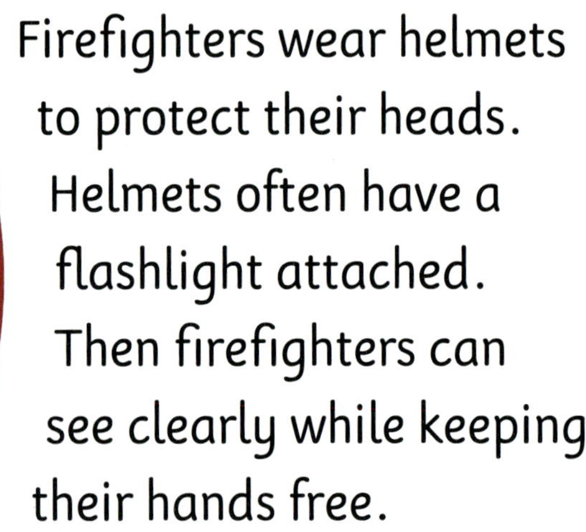

Firefighters wear helmets to protect their heads. Helmets often have a flashlight attached. Then firefighters can see clearly while keeping their hands free.

Firefighters carry oxygen cylinders full of air on their backs. The cylinders are connected to face masks. This equipment helps firefighters breathe.

DID YOU KNOW?

Each cylinder gives firefighters 30 to 45 minutes of air.

A HISTORY OF FIREFIGHTING

Around 2,000 Years Ago
The first fire brigade was started in Rome. It was called the Vigiles.

The Early 1700s
Early fire engines were carts. The water was pumped out by hand.

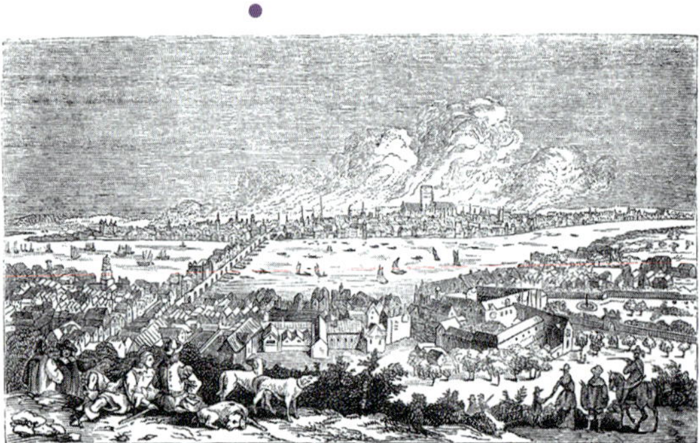

1666
The Great Fire of London started in a bakery. It burned down most of the city. After this, a firefighting system was created in England.

1736
Benjamin Franklin helped create the first American fire department. The firefighters were all volunteers.

1853
In the United States, firefighting became a paid job for the first time.

1902
The first motorized fire vehicles were used in the United States. Soon many cities had motorized fire engines.

BECOMING A FIREFIGHTER

Firefighters must be at least 18 years old.

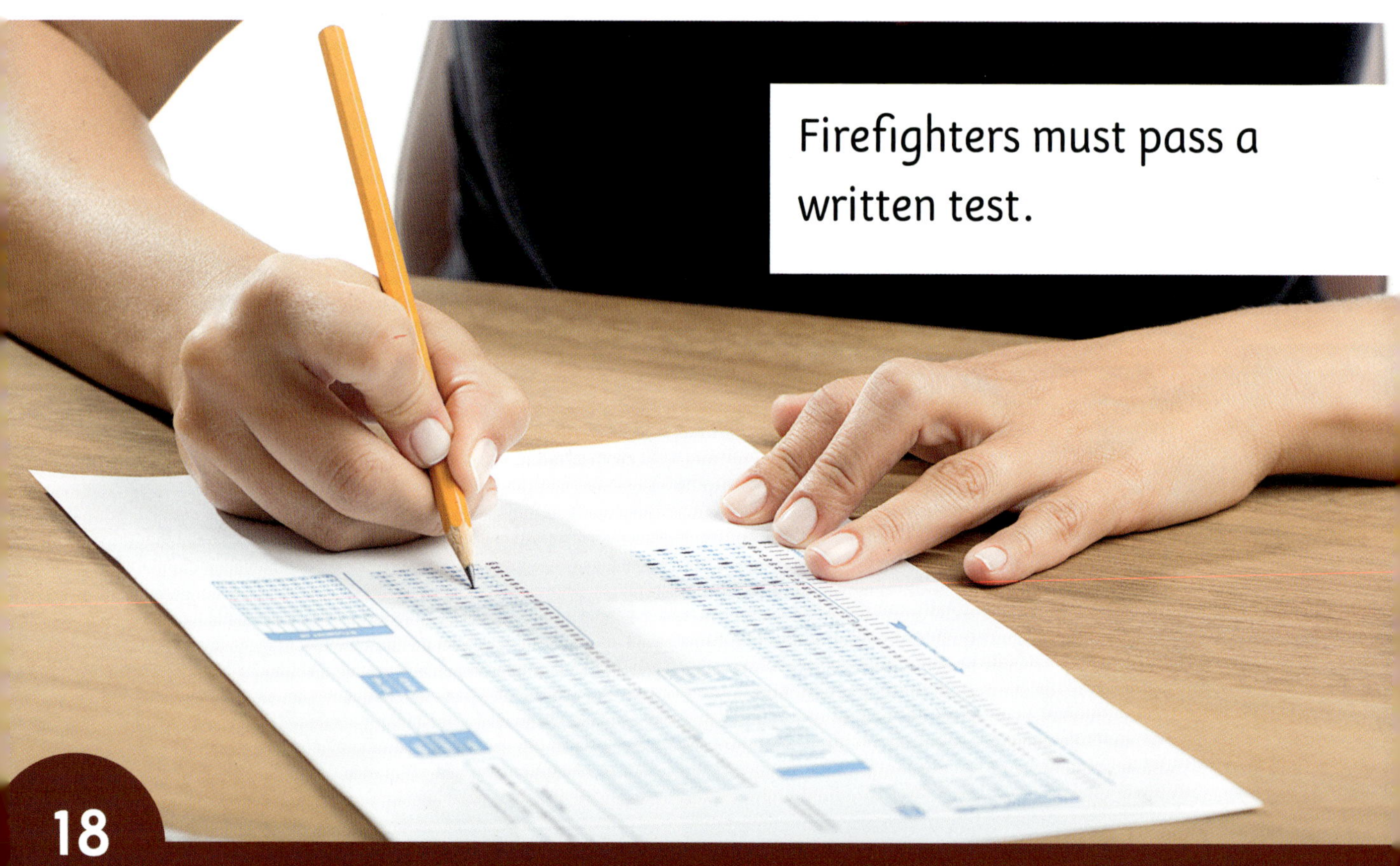

Firefighters must pass a written test.

It takes a lot of training to become a firefighter. Most firefighters attend fire academies. Others may become an apprentice.

Firefighters need to pass fitness tests to get the job. They have to run, climb, lift heavy equipment, and much more.

BELIEVE IT OR NOT!

President George Washington was a volunteer firefighter in Virginia when he was young.

The gear a firefighter wears is very heavy. It can weigh between 45 and 75 pounds (20 and 34 kg).

Dalmatians were once used as fire station dogs. They ran ahead of the fire carts and barked to clear the road.

Before firefighters had powerful hoses, they fought fires by pulling buildings down with hooks. Stopping the fire from spreading was more important than saving the building.

ARE YOU A GENIUS KID?

Now you know many things about firefighters. Your friends and family are going to be amazed! But how much can you remember? It's time for a quiz!

Check back through the book if you are not sure.

1. Why do firefighters need ladders?
2. What are the three things needed for a fire to start?
3. Who helped create the first American fire department?

Answers:
1. To get to places up high, 2. Oxygen, fuel, and heat, 3. Benjamin Franklin.

GLOSSARY

apprentice someone who works for someone else to learn a skill or trade

community a group of people who are connected by something

dispatcher a person whose job is to take emergency calls and send police, ambulance, or firefighters out to that emergency

equipment items that are needed to complete a certain job

fire extinguishers tanks containing a chemical that can be sprayed on a fire to put it out

first aid emergency medical help that is given to someone until an ambulance arrives

natural disasters natural events, such as earthquakes or floods, that cause serious damage and loss of life

oxygen a natural gas that living things need in order to live

INDEX